How ___ in cows?

Written by Emily Hooton
Illustrated by Noah Warnes

Collins

How far is the moon?

A rocket can zoom to the moon in less than a week.

If you run, you might get to the moon in 4.5 years!

4

A cow might run that far in 1.5 years!

How far is it to Mars?

6

A cow might run to Mars in 940 years.
Or longer if it has a nap.

Mars

225,000,000 km

No cow has been that far!

Yet!

How long are my guts?

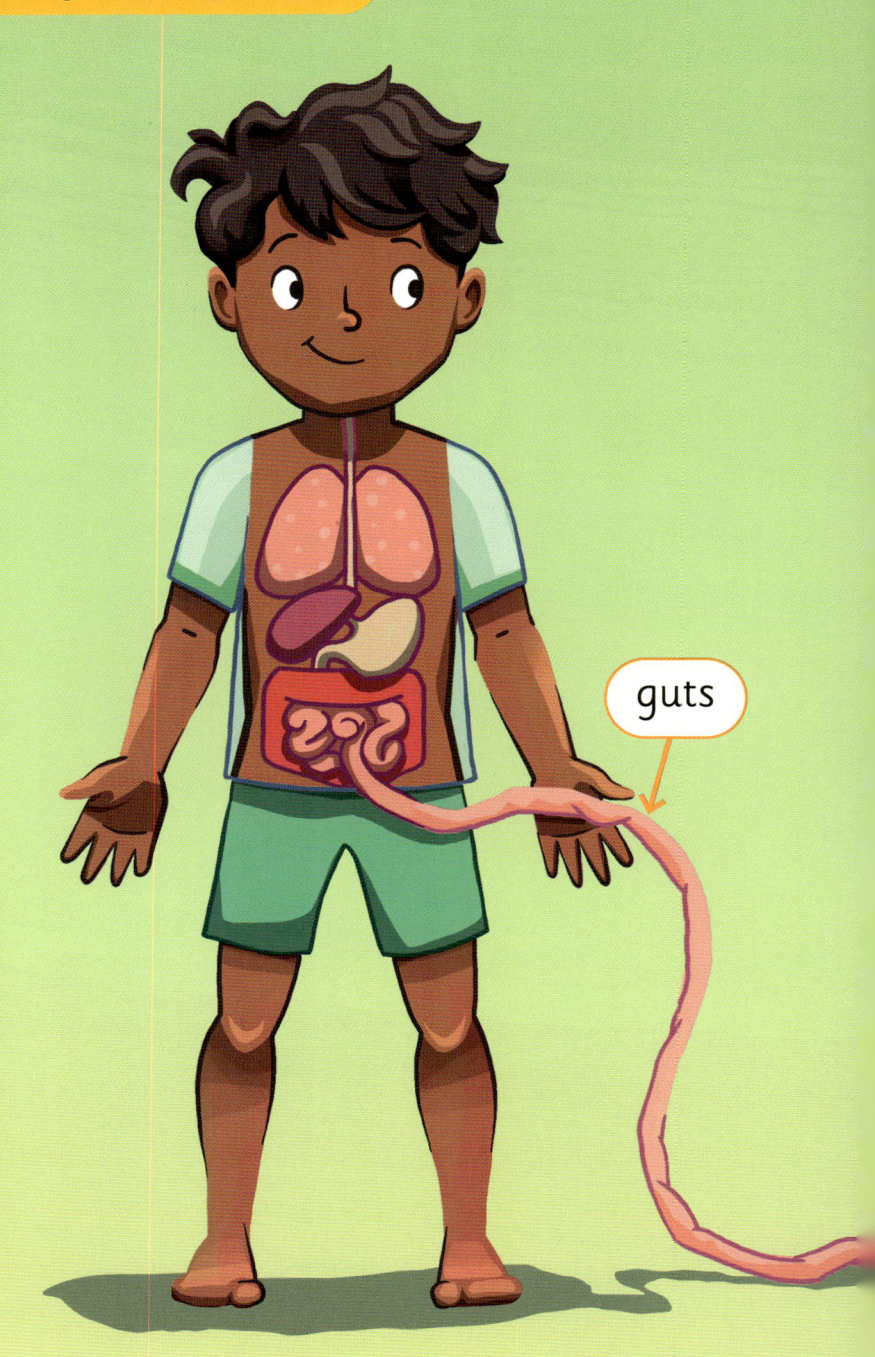

guts

10

Guts are as long as 16 cats put tip to tail ... or 3 cows!

2.5 m

11

How high is it?

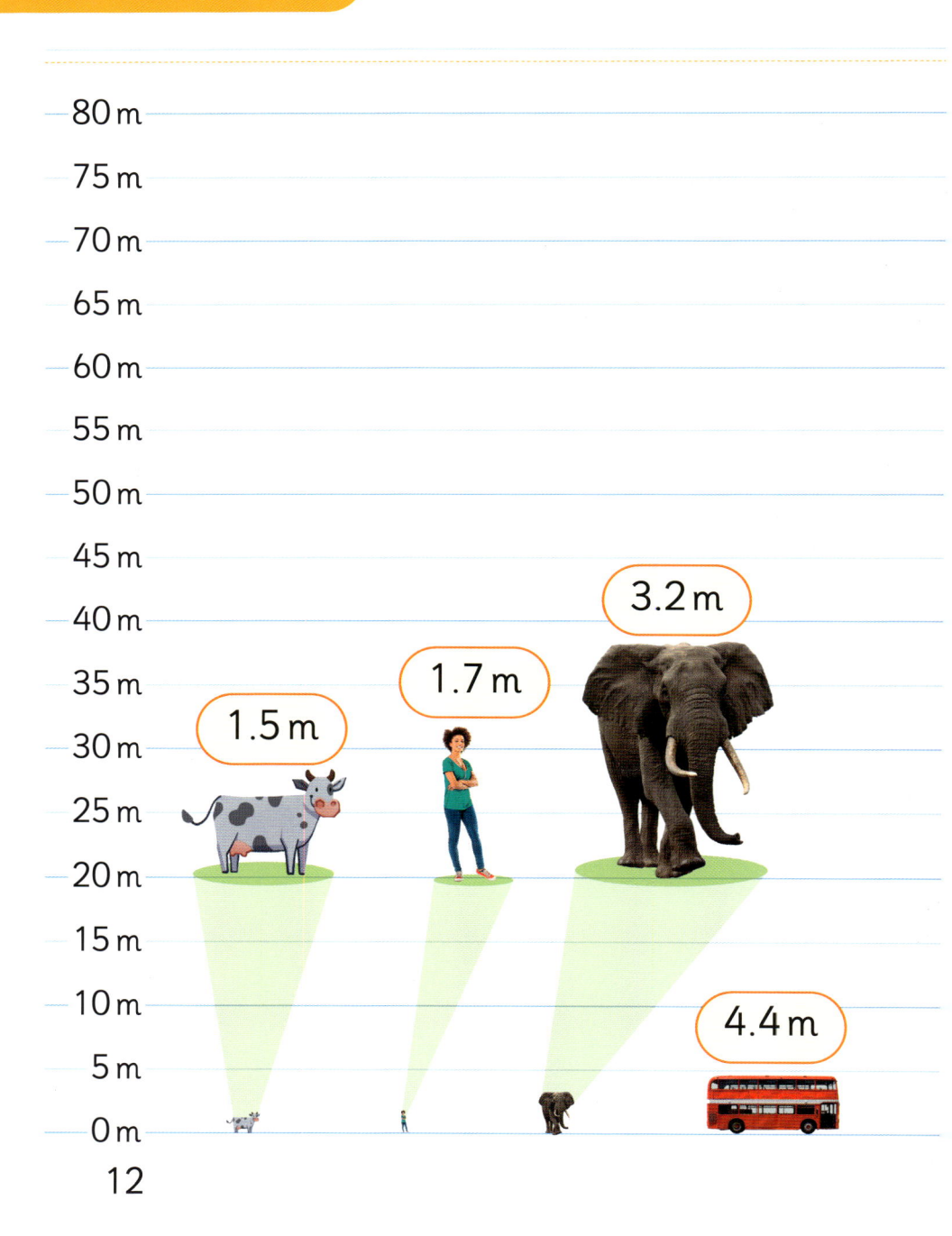

- 80 m
- 75 m
- 70 m
- 65 m
- 60 m
- 55 m
- 50 m
- 45 m
- 40 m
- 35 m
- 30 m
- 25 m
- 20 m
- 15 m
- 10 m
- 5 m
- 0 m

1.5 m

1.7 m

3.2 m

4.4 m

redwood 84 m ... or 56 cows

30 m

13

Are mushrooms as big as cows?

No!

But the roots of this fungus are 4,000 cows long!

How far in cows?

16

moon

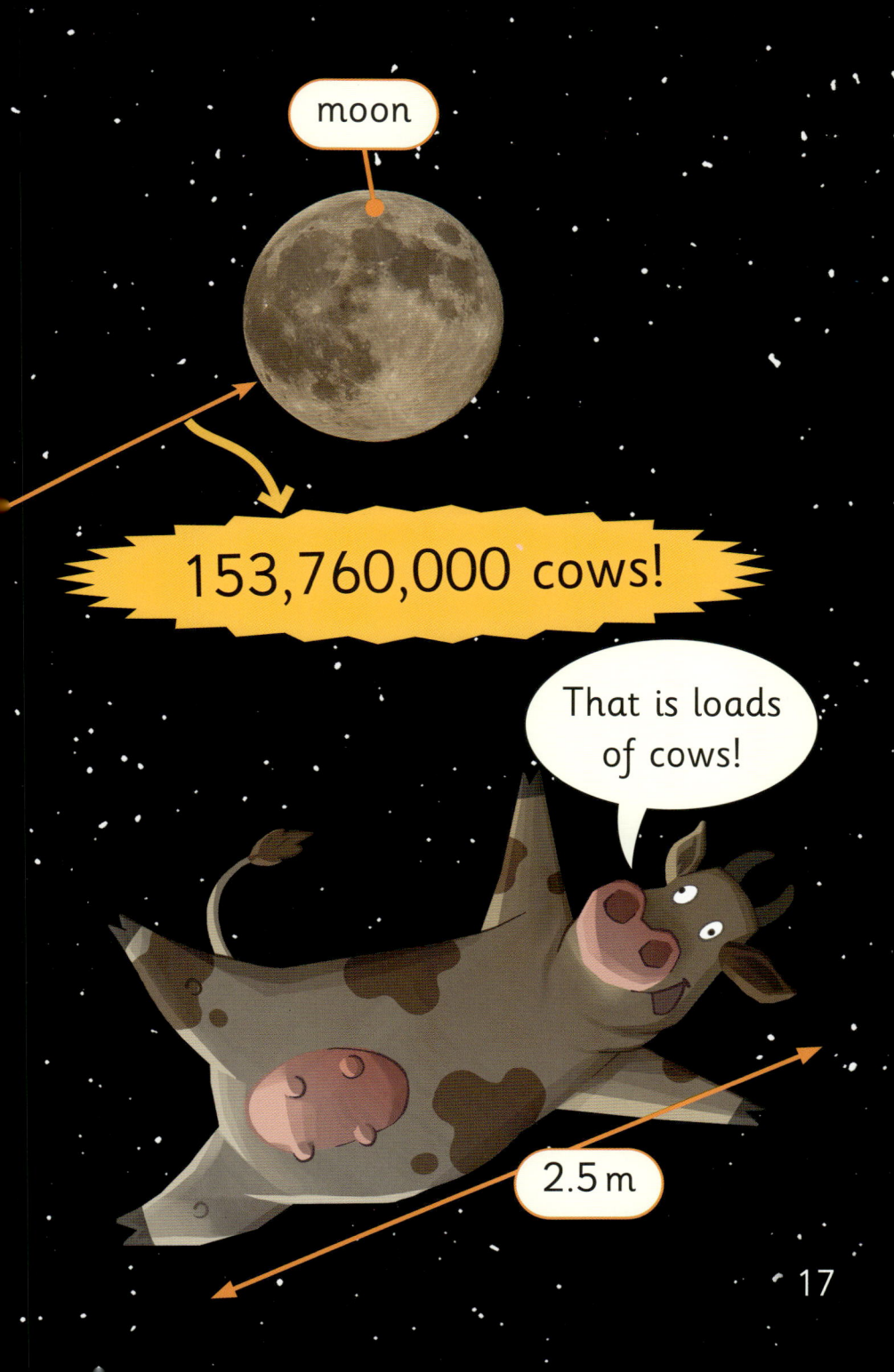

153,760,000 cows!

That is loads of cows!

2.5 m

How long in cows?

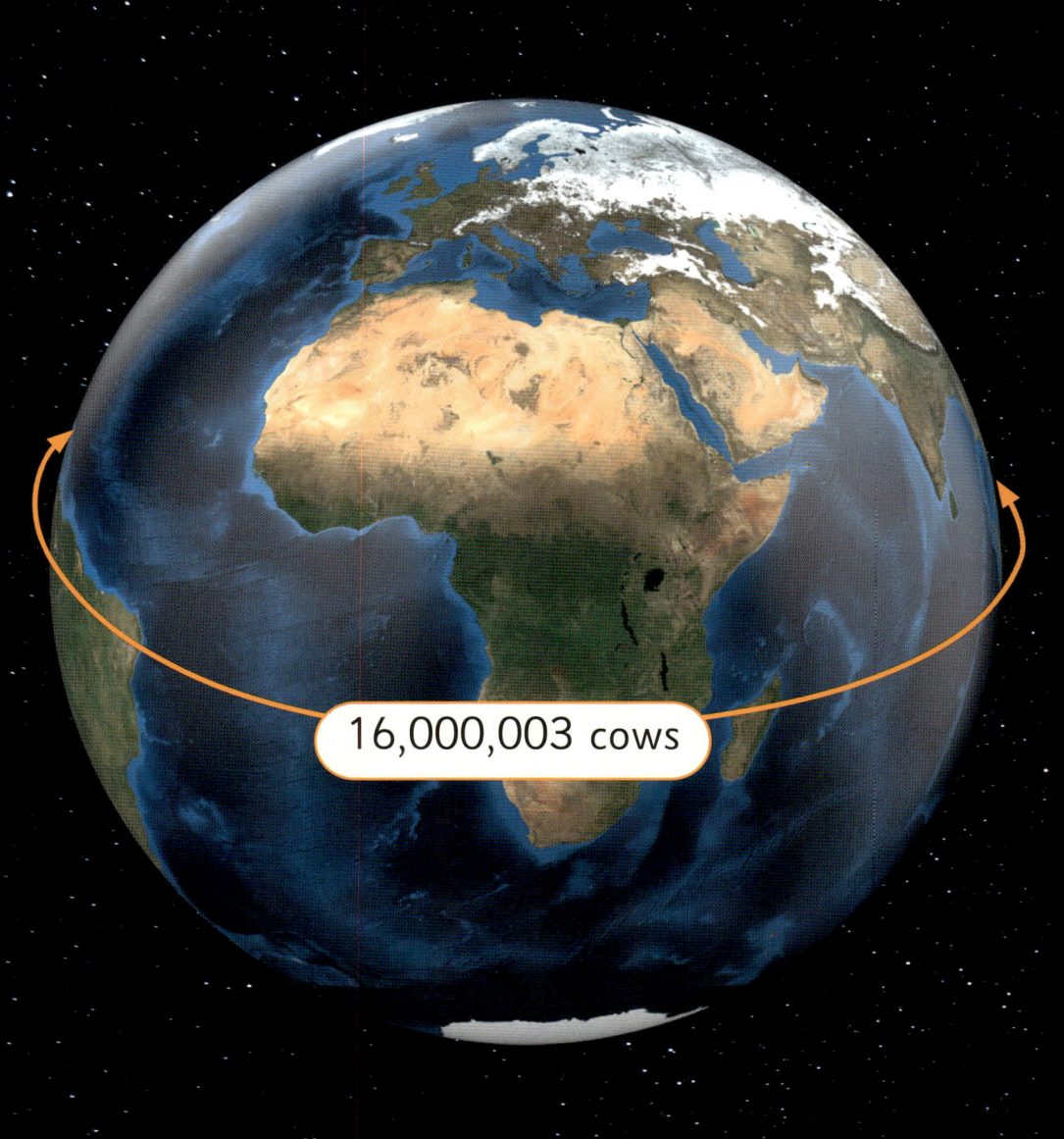

16,000,003 cows

2.5 m

How high is the Shard?

1.5 m

206 cows

Wow!

1.5 m

2.5 m

84 m

3.2 m

22

10 km

7.5 m

🐾 Review: After reading 🐾

Use your assessment from hearing the children read to choose any GPCs, words or tricky words that need additional practice.

Read 1: Decoding
- Ask the children to read pages 4 and 5. Encourage them to blend in their heads, silently, before reading the words aloud. Focus on the word **might**. Ask: Why do you think the author uses **might** and not **will** on these pages? (e.g. *because it's not certain – neither you nor the cow are likely to be able to run through space!*)
- Ask the children to sound out these words. Ask: Which two or three letters make one sound in each of the words?

years (*ear*)	**zoom** (*oo*)	**week** (*ee*)
tail (*ai*)	**longer** (*ng, er*)	**cow** (*ow*)

Read 2: Prosody
- Turn to pages 10 and 11. Discuss how you would read these pages to get a jokey tone across.
  - Encourage the children to choose the funniest word to emphasise. (e.g. *guts*)
  - Focus on page 11. What tone might they use for the first answer? (e.g. *lively*) Which word should they emphasise in the last part of the sentence? (e.g. *cows – because it links with the title of the book*)
- Turn to pages 14 and 15. Encourage the children to read the pages aloud in the voice of a documentary narrator. Can they use different tones to hold the attention of the listeners?

Read 3: Comprehension
- Ask the children to think of as many units as they can that are usually used to measure speed, distance and length. Discuss which units are used in a car, or in space or at school.
- On page 8, 225 million kilometres is the average distance from Earth to Mars. Discuss with the children why the distance might change. (e.g. *the distance changes as the planets orbit the sun*)
- Bonus content: Turn to pages 16 and 17. Ask: Why is page 17 funny? Do you think it is funnier to measure in cows, instead of other units of measure? Why?
- Turn to pages 22 and 23 and talk about how else each of these measurements could be described. (e.g. *numbers of cows or cats*) Ask: What sort of measures are more memorable? Why?